MW00647632

Tax Free Wealth

Learn the strategies and loopholes of the wealthy on lowering taxes by leveraging Cash Value Life Insurance, 1031 Real Estate Exchanges, 401k & IRA Investing

By

Income Mastery

cause the resulting actions to be solely within his or her competence. There are no scenarios in which the publisher or author of this book can be held responsible for any difficulties or damages that may occur to them after making the information presented here.

In addition, the information on the following pages is intended to be for informational purposes only and should therefore be regarded as universal. As befits its nature, it is presented without warranty with respect to its prolonged validity or provisional quality. The trademarks mentioned are made without written consent and can in no way be considered as sponsorship of the same.

Table of Contents

Chapter 1: Cash Value Insurance and the Road to Wealth

What is Cash Value Insurance? Can it help us increase our wealth?

Permanent life insurance is a general term for life insurance plans that do not expire, unlike term life insurance, which promises payment of a specified death benefit within a specified period of years.

Permanent life insurance usually combines a death benefit with a savings amount, allowing policies to generate a cash value which allows the owner to borrow funds or, in some cases, withdraw cash to help meet needs such as paying for a child's college education or covering medical expenses.

How does cash value life insurance work?

Cash value insurance is permanent life insurance because it provides coverage for the life of the insured. Traditionally, cash value life insurance has higher premiums than term insurance because of the cash value element. Most cash value life insurance policies require a fixed level premium payment, of which an amount is assigned to the cost of the insurance and the rest is deposited into a cash value account.

The cash value of life insurance generates a modest interest rate, with deferred taxes on accumulated earnings. Therefore, the cash value of life insurance will increase over time.

What are the differences, why is it important, and how do you understand cash value life insurance?

Cash value life insurance is more expensive than term life insurance. Unlike temporary life insurance, cash value policies do not expire after a specified number of years. It is possible to borrow against a cash value life insurance policy.

As the cash value increases, the insurance company's risk decreases as the accumulated cash value offsets some of the insurer's liability. For example, consider a policy with a death benefit of $25,000. The policy has no prior outstanding loans or cash withdrawals and an accumulated cash value of $5,000. At the insured's death, the insurance company pays the total death benefit of $25,000. The money collected on the cash value is now the property of the insurer. Because the cash value is $5,000, the actual liability cost to the insurance company is $20,000 ($25,000-$5,000).

Whole life, variable life and universal life insurance are examples of cash value life insurance. Some provide cash value as a benefit to the alive policyholder. The cash value component serves only as a vital benefit to policyholders. As a vital benefit, the insured may resort to any cash value during his lifetime. There are several options for accessing funds. For most policies, partial or full withdrawals are allowed.

The net cash value of life insurance is what you or your beneficiaries have left once the insurance company deducts fees or any expenses incurred during the ownership of the policy.

Taxes are deferred on earnings until they are withdrawn from the policy and distributed. Once distributed, earnings are taxed at the policyholder's standard tax rate. Some policies allow unlimited withdrawals, while others restrict how many drawings can be taken during a calendar period or year. In addition, some policies limit the amounts available for elimination (e.g., a minimum of $500).

Most cash value life insurance arrangements allow cash value loans. Like any other loan, the issuer will charge interest on the outstanding principal. The outstanding loan amount will reduce the dollar-for-dollar death benefit in the event of the death of the policyholder prior to full loan repayment. Some insurers require repayment of loan interest and, if it is not paid, may deduct interest from the remaining cash value. The cash value can also be used to pay policy premiums. If there is enough cash value, an insured can stop paying premiums out of pocket and have the cash value account cover the payment.

Chapter 2: What is Cash Value Insurance? Learn about it and how it benefits you.

Let's start by explaining Cash Value Insurance. Have you ever heard of it? Here's what Cash Value Insurance is and how it works. Cash Value Insurance is a permanent life insurance that includes a savings component. Permanent life insurance is a general term for life insurance plans that do not expire, unlike term life insurance, which promises payment of a specific death benefit within a specific period of years. We must take this into account in order to understand how it works and how it will benefit you.

Permanent life insurance usually combines a death benefit for the person who is the policyholder along with an amount of savings, which is what allows policies to generate cash value. This means that only the policyholder can borrow funds or even withdraw cash. For example, you could ask for this cash in order to pay for your children's college education, cover different types of medical expenses, or situations that require cash.

Cash Value Life Insurance is permanent life insurance which provides coverage for the life of the insured. Traditionally, Cash Value Life Insurance has higher premiums than term insurance because of the cash value element. Most Cash Value Life Insurance policies require a fixed premium payment, as a portion of this premium is allocated to the cost of the insurance and the rest is deposited into a cash value account. This is what gives us that cash we can use in an emergency. Remember that you must always have cash and/or emergency savings, whether it is an emergency fund which you will be able to use in case of an emergency or some expenses which were not programmed.

In addition, Cash Value Life Insurance generates a modest, tax-deferred interest rate on accumulated earnings. Therefore, the cash value of life insurance will increase over time.

Why is Cash Value Life Insurance good for you? How does it help reduce your taxes and increase the money you have available? What are the differences between Cash Value Life Insurance and traditional insurance?

Cash Value Life Insurance is more expensive than term life insurance because it has many more benefits. For example, unlike temporary life insurance, cash value policies do not expire after a specified number of years. It is possible to borrow against a cash value life insurance policy. This will benefit us in case we want to make big purchases, by having this extra cash, you can avoid getting into debt. This will also help us have a better credit line in case we want to ask for important loans such as a house or an apartment loan therefore this is going to help us qualify for it.

So, we'll explain how this kind of insurance works. As Cash Value Life Insurance increases, the insurance company's risk decreases, as the accumulated cash value offsets some of the insurer's liability. What do we mean by this? Consider for example a policy with a death benefit of $25,000. The policy has no prior outstanding loans or cash withdrawals and an accumulated cash value of $5,000. At the insured's death, the insurance company pays the total death benefit of $25,000. The money collected on the cash value is now the property of the insurer. Because the cash value is $5,000, the actual liability cost to the insurance company is $20,000 ($25,000-$5,000).

We must keep in mind that the cash value we can withdraw is a benefit only for the policyholder, i.e. the cash value component serves only as a benefit for policyholders. As a vital benefit, the insured may resort to any cash value during his lifetime. There are several options available to the policyholder for withdrawing funds and accessing funds. For most policies, partial fund deliveries or withdrawals are permitted.

We should keep in mind that the net cash value of life insurance is what the policyholder or their beneficiaries have left once the insurance company deducts their fees or any expenses incurred.

It should be noted that taxes are deferred on earnings until they are withdrawn from the policy and distributed. Once distributed, earnings are taxed at the policyholder's standard tax rate. Some policies allow unlimited withdrawals, while others restrict how many drawings can be taken during a calendar period or year. In addition, some policies limit the amounts available for elimination (e.g., a minimum of $500).

Most cash value life insurance arrangements allow cash value loans. Like any other loan, the issuer will charge interest on the outstanding principal. The outstanding loan amount will reduce the dollar-for-dollar death benefit in the event of the death of the policyholder prior to full loan repayment. Some insurers require repayment of loan interest and, if it is not paid, may deduct interest from the remaining cash value. The cash value can also be used to pay policy premiums. If there is enough cash value, an insured can stop paying premiums out of pocket and have the cash value account cover the payment.

Chapter 3: 1031 Real Estate Exchanges, what is it?

In a field loaded with specialized terminology, it is essential to begin by understanding the basics.

A Real Estate Exchange 1031 is named after Section 1031 of the Internal Revenue Code of the United States which allows you to avoid paying capital gain taxes when you sell investment property and reinvest the proceeds of the sale within certain time limits in property or properties of a similar type and equal or greater value.

Under section 1031, any proceeds received from the sale of a property remain taxable. For that reason, the proceeds of the sale should be transferred to a qualified intermediary, rather than the seller of the property, and the qualified intermediary transfers them to the seller of the replacement property or properties. A qualified intermediary is a person or company that agrees to facilitate the 1031 exchange by holding the funds involved in the transaction until they can be transferred to the seller of the replacement property. The qualified intermediary cannot have any other formal relationship with the parties exchanging goods.

As an investor, there are several reasons why you might consider using a 1031 exchange. Some of these reasons include:

a) You are looking for a property that has better return prospects or you want to diversify your assets.

b) If you own real estate, you may be looking for a managed property rather than managing it yourself.

c) You may want to consolidate several properties into one, for estate planning purposes, or you may want to divide a single property into several assets.

d) Reset the amortization clock (explained below).

The main benefit of doing a 1031 exchange rather than simply selling one property and buying another is tax deferral, meaning tax reduction. A 1031 exchange allows you to defer capital gains tax, freeing up more capital for investment in replacement property. This will help you to have more wealth, that is to say, to have more income and to deduct your taxes.

However, it is important to keep in mind that a 1031 exchange may require a high minimum investment and maintenance time. This makes these transactions more ideal for people with higher net worth. Due to their complexity, 1031 exchange transactions must be handled by professionals. Let's remember that we must follow certain rules, and even though there are different strategies and shortcuts to reduce our taxes, we must always comply with the rules.

Now, let's continue talking and explaining what depreciation is and why it is important for a 1031 exchange.

Depreciation is an essential concept which allows you to understand the true benefits of an exchange 1031. But what does it mean and what does it represent? Depreciation is the percentage of the cost of an investment property that is written off each year, recognizing the effects of wear and tear. In other words, every year we must depreciate the property due to wear and tear. When a property is sold, capital gains taxes are calculated based on the adjusted net base of the property, which reflects the original purchase price of the property, plus capital improvements less depreciation. This amount must be taken into account since we will have to deduce it annually.

If a property is sold for more than its depreciated value, you may have to recoup the depreciation. That means that the amount of the depreciation will be included in your taxable income from the sale of the property.

Since the size of recaptured depreciation increases over time, you may be motivated to participate in a 1031 exchange to avoid the large increase in taxable income that recovery from depreciation would cause later. The recovery of depreciation will be a factor to consider when calculating the value of any 1031 exchange transaction.

On the other hand, the choice of a replacement property is vital, there are certain rules and time we must follow in order to apply 1031 and reduce our taxes.

Property of a similar type is defined according to its nature or characteristics, not by its quality or grade. This means that there is a wide range of real interchangeable properties. Vacant land can be exchanged for a commercial building, for example, or industrial property can be exchanged for residential. We must be clear about what is interchangeable and what is not. For example, real estate cannot be exchanged for work of art, as this does not meet the definition of a similar type. However, the property must be kept for investment, not for resale or personal use. This usually involves a minimum of two years of ownership. We must highlight that the property must be maintained for investment, not for resale or personal use.

To receive the full benefit of a 1031 exchange, your replacement property must be of equal or of greater value. You must identify a replacement property for assets sold within forty-five days and then complete the exchange within one hundred and eighty days. There are three rules that can be applied. You must comply with one of the following:

1) The rule of three properties allows you to identify three properties as potential purchases, regardless of their market value.

2) The two hundred percent rule allows you to identify unlimited replacement properties as long as their accumulated value does not exceed two hundred percent of the value of the property sold. We must take this percentage very seriously when making decisions.

3) The ninety-five percent rule allows you to identify as many properties as you want as long as you acquire properties valued at ninety-five percent of their total value or more.

There are several possibilities for 1031 exchanges, these will vary in time and other details, each will create a set of requirements and procedures to be followed. Remember that you must follow the law and we must fully abide it. Now, we must see which one suits you and which one we could fit in and what we can use and how we can use it to our advantage.

1) 1031 exchanges within one hundred and eighty days are commonly known as delayed exchanges because, at one time, the exchanges had to take place simultaneously.

2) Custom construction exchanges allow the replacement property on a 1031 exchange to be renovated or newly constructed. However, these types of exchanges are still subject to the 180-day time rule, which means that all improvements and construction must be completed by the time the transaction is completed. Any subsequent improvements are considered personal property

and will not qualify as part of the exchange. Take this time into account in order to qualify.

3) If you acquire replacement property before selling the property to be exchanged, it is called reverse exchange. In this case, the property must be transferred to an exchange accommodation holder (who may be the qualified intermediary) and a qualified exchange accommodation agreement must be signed. Within forty-five days after the transfer of the property, a property must be identified for exchange and the transaction must be made within one hundred and eighty days.

We always recommend consulting with an expert. We must consider the number of days and that we meet the conditions. Remember, if we don't comply, we won't be able to apply or qualify for 1031.

Properties of a similar type in an exchange must also have a similar value. The difference in value between a property and the property being exchanged is called a boot. We would like to emphasize that they must have a similar value.

If a replacement property is of less value than the property sold, the difference (cash start) is subject to tax. If personal property or dissimilar property is used to complete the transaction, it will be initiated, but take into consideration that this does not disqualify it to become a 1031 exchange.

The presence of a mortgage is allowed on both sides of the exchange. If the replacement mortgage is less than the mortgage on the property being sold, the difference is treated as a cash boot. That fact should be taken into account when calculating the parameters of the exchange.

Expenses and tariffs affect the value of the transaction and therefore also the potential start-up. Some expenses can be paid with exchange funds. These include:

- • Runner's commissions
- • Qualified Intermediate Rates
- • Presentation fees
- • Related Attorney Fees
- • Title insurance premiums
- • Related Tax Advisor Fees
- • Search Engine Rates
- • Deposit fees

Expenses that cannot be paid with exchange funds include:

- • Financing rates
- • Property Taxes
- • Repair or maintenance costs.
- • Insurance premiums

Chapter 4: Partner Exchanges: Drop and Swap 1031 Exchanges

LLCs can only exchange property as an entity, in case some partners want to make an exchange and others don't.

The interest in a partnership cannot be used in a 1031 exchange: the partners in an LLC do not own the property, they own a proprietary entity, which is the taxpayer of the property. You have to keep this in mind. 1031 exchanges are made by a single taxpayer as one side of the transaction. Therefore, special steps are required when members of an LLC or partnership do not agree with the disposition of property. This can be quite complex because each owner's situation is unique, but the basics are universal.

When one partner wants to do a 1031 exchange and the others don't, that partner can transfer the partnership's interests to the LLC in exchange for a deed at an equivalent percentage of ownership. This makes the partner a tenant in common with the LLC, and a separate taxpayer. When the LLC's property is sold, that partner's share of the profits goes to a qualified intermediary, while the other partners receive theirs directly.

When most members wish to participate in a 1031 exchange, dissenting members may receive a certain percentage of the property at the time of the transaction and pay income taxes while the income of others goes to a qualified intermediary. This procedure is called "release and exchange" and it is the most common procedure in these situations.

A 1031 exchange can also be made on properties held for investment. An important "holding for investment" diagnosis is the amount of time an asset is held. It is desirable to initiate the (member's) fall at least one year prior to the exchange of the asset. Otherwise, the Internal Revenue Service (IRS) may see that the partners participating in the exchange do not meet that criterion. If that is not possible, the exchange can take place first and partners who want to do so can leave after a reasonable interval. This is known as an "exchange and release".

Chapter 5: Leasing Common Property Exchanges

Like drop and swap, common holding exchanges are another variation of 1031 transactions. Tenancy in common is not a joint venture or partnership (which would not be allowed to participate in a 1031 exchange), but it is a relationship that allows you to have a fractional interest directly in a large property, along with one for thirty-four persons and more entities. This allows relatively small investors to participate in a transaction, in addition to having a number of other applications in 1031 exchanges.

Strictly speaking, tenure in common gives investors the ability to own real estate with other owners, but to have the same rights as a single owner. Tenants in common do not need permission from other tenants to buy or sell their share of the property, but they often must meet certain financial requirements to be credited.

Tenure in common can be used to divide or consolidate financial holdings, diversify holdings, or obtain a share in a much larger asset. Allows you to specify the volume of investment in a single project, which is important in a 1031 exchange, where the value of one asset must match the other one.

Now, how does 1031 affect estate planning?

One of the main benefits of participating in a 1031 exchange is that you can take that tax deferment to the grave. If your heirs inherit the property received through a 1031 exchange, its value is "raised" to the fair market, which cancels the tax deferral debt. Let's keep this information in mind as it lowers our taxes, raises the value of property and leads us to the path of wealth.

This means that if you die without having sold the property obtained through a 1031 exchange, the heirs receive it at the increased market rate value, and all deferred taxes are erased. An estate planner should be consulted to make the most of this opportunity. Tenancy in common can be used to structure assets according to your wishes for distribution after death. This is a very good option for not having to pay high taxes when children are inheriting property.

The tax deferral provided by a 1031 exchange is a wonderful opportunity for investors. Although complex in certain points, these complexities allow for great flexibility. This is not a procedure for an investor acting alone. Competent professional assistance is required in virtually every step.

Chapter 5: 401K: What is a 401(k) plan? How does this type of plan benefit us?

A 401(k) plan is a defined contribution retirement account with tax advantages that many employers offer their employees. It is named after a section of the U.S. Internal Revenue Code. Workers can make contributions to their 401(k) accounts through automatic payroll withholding, and their employers can match some or all of those contributions. Gains from investing in a traditional 401(k) plan are not taxed until the employee withdraws that money, usually after retirement. In a Roth 401(k) plan, withdrawals may be tax-free. This helps us save for our retirement in a voluntary and orderly manner. This is going to help us because our employees are not going to give us the total of our salary, they are going to deduct the amount that we want to contribute for our retirement. This will make it easier for us to save and organize our expenses. We recommend that you talk to your employer and see if you can contribute to your retirement.

So, we should think of the 401(k) plan as a company-sponsored retirement account to which employees can contribute. Employers may also make matching contributions.

There are two basic types of 401(k), traditional and Roth, which differ mainly in how they are taxed. Keep this difference in mind before you talk to your employer. Below we explain the differences between the traditional 401 (k) and Roth.

In a traditional 401(k), employee contributions reduce their income taxes during the year in which they are made, but their withdrawals are taxable. With a Roth, employees make contributions with after-tax income, but can make tax-free withdrawals. Now, in order to understand in depth, the difference between the plans, we must make the following remarks.

There are two 401 (k) plans, meaning that we must keep in mind that there are two basic types of 401 (k) accounts; the regular 401 (k) and the traditional Roth 401 (k), sometimes referred to as "designated Roth accounts. The two are similar in many ways, but they are taxed in different ways. A worker may have either type of account or may even have both. We must analyze them so that we can compare them and decide what is going to be the best option for us.

Chapter 5: Contributing to a 401(k) plan:

Now that you know what the 401(k) plan is, we explain how to make contributions. Let's start with the 401(k). This is known as a defined contribution plan. The employee and employer may make contributions to the account, up to the dollar limit established by the Internal Revenue Service (IRS). In contrast, traditional pensions (not to be confused with traditional 401(k)) are called defined benefit plans; this means that the employer is responsible for providing a specific amount of money to the employee at retirement. This has already been agreed. In recent decades, 401(k) plans have become more abundant and traditional pensions are increasingly rare, as employers have transferred the responsibility and risk of saving for retirement to their employees.

Employees are also responsible for choosing specific investments within their 401(k) accounts from their employer's selection. Those offerings generally include a variety of stock and bond mutual funds, as well as target date funds that have a combination of stocks and bonds appropriate in terms of risk for when that person expects to retire. They may also include guaranteed investment contracts (GICs) issued by insurance companies and, sometimes, the employer's own shares. This, as you may have seen, takes the pressure off the employer and takes away the responsibility to provide a specific amount of money to the employee at retirement.

The maximum amount an employee or employer can contribute to a 401(k) plan is periodically adjusted for inflation. It's very important that we keep this in mind. Beginning in 2019, the basic limits on employee contributions are nineteen thousand U.S. dollars per year for workers under the age of fifty and twenty-five thousand for those over fifty. If the employer also contributes (or if the employee chooses to make additional non-deductible after-tax contributions to his or her traditional 401(k) account), the employee's and/or employer's total contribution for workers under age fifty is limited to fifty-six thousand U.S. dollars or one hundred percent of the employees' compensation, whichever is less. For those over the age of fifty, the limit is sixty-two thousand US dollars. You need to consider your age to calculate how much you could save with the 401(k). We also recommend that you take into account the years to come so that you can see what is going to suit you. We recommend that you consider all the information, take a couple of hours, a couple of days and do the full research to decide what really suits you.

Employers that match their employees' contributions use different formulas to calculate that match. A common example might be fifty cents or one dollar for every dollar the employee contributes up to a certain percentage of the salary. Financial advisors often recommend that employees try to contribute at least enough money to their 401(k) plans to obtain full employer matching. You must remember that you will receive this money when you retire, you will have to make an effort to be able to have more wealth and less worries.

Participants should remember that once their money is in a 401(k), it can be difficult to withdraw without penalty. Remember, you may have emergency expenses. You must have a monthly, including a weekly budget that includes 401(k) contributions, an emergency fund, money for your expenses, and money to save. We also recommend that you look for a 401(k) where you can easily access only if it is necessary., otherwise, we recommend that you do not withdraw any money from the 401(k).

If they wish, and if their employer offers both options, employees can split their contributions, putting some money into a traditional 401(k) and some into a Roth 401(k). However, your total contribution to both types of accounts cannot exceed the limit for one account (such as nineteen thousand in 2019). Employers' contributions can only go into a traditional 401(k) account, where they will be taxable at retirement.

Chapter 6: Taking Withdrawals from a 401(k) Plan

Profits in a 401(k) account are tax-deferred in the case of the traditional 401(k) and tax-free in the case of Roth's. When the owner of a traditional 401(k) makes withdrawals, that money (which has never been taxed) will be taxed as ordinary income. Owners of Roth accounts (who have already paid income taxes on the money they contributed to the plan) will not be required to pay taxes on their withdrawals, as long as they meet certain requirements. Take this into account to see what kind of plan is right for you.

Both traditional and Roth 401(k) owners must be at least fifty-nine and six months old, or meet other criteria set by the Internal Revenue Service (IRS), such as being totally and permanently disabled, will allow them to begin making withdrawals. Otherwise, they will face an additional ten percent pre-distribution penalty tax in addition to any other taxes they owe. For this reason, we emphasize the importance of having a budget, of having an emergency fund and of having savings. We must have our finances in order, we must consider our expenses and our income. Try to cut as many unnecessary expenses as possible, this will increase the amount of money available to spend or save. Do not withdraw it unless it is absolutely necessary, that is for a really urgent issue such as health for example. We would recommend know your expenses, your income in order to draw up a budget and follow it.

Now, consider that both types of accounts are also subject to required minimum distributions or RMDs. (Withdrawals are often referred to as "distributions" in the language of the Internal Revenue Service.) After age seventy and six months, account owners must withdraw at least a specified percentage of their 401(k) plans, using IRS tables based on their life expectancy at that time. However, if they are still working and the account is with their current employer, they may not have to take RMDs from that plan. (Roth IRAs, unlike Roth 401(k), are not subject to RMDs during the owner's useful life.) You must think until what age you want to work because this will affect your retirement plan.

Chapter 7: More Differences between Traditional 401(k) and Roth 401(k)

When 401(k) plans first became available in 1978, companies and their employees had only one option: the traditional 401(k). Then, in 2006, came Roth 401 (k) s. The Roth is named after former U.S. Senator William Roth of Delaware, the main sponsor of the 1997 legislation that made the Roth IRA possible.

While Roth 401(k) was a bit slow to catch up, many employers now offer them. So, the first decision that employees usually make is: Roth or traditional? What are the differences, and which one is right for me? You must ask yourself which of the two will take you to tranquility and increase your wealth.

Let's start, as a general rule, employees who expect to be in a lower marginal tax bracket after retirement can opt for a traditional 401(k) and take advantage of the immediate tax exemption. On the other hand, employees who expect to be in a higher rank could opt for the Roth so they can avoid taxes later. For example, a Roth might be the right choice for a younger worker whose salary is relatively low now but is likely to increase substantially over time. It's also important, to take this into consideration no tax on withdrawals means that all money earned by contributions over decades of being in the account is also not taxable. Take this information into account so that you can make the right decision that will benefit you over time.

Since no one can predict what tax rates will be within decades, none of the 401(k) rates are safe. For that reason, many financial advisors suggest that people cover their bets, putting some of their money into each. This can be done and will make you benefit from both parties, as neither is safe.

You must have some special considerations which are going to affect the plan. For example, a change of job is what most affects the plan. So, when an employee leaves a company where he or she has a 401(k) plan, he or she usually has four options:

1. Withdraw the money

This is often a bad idea unless the employee really needs the cash for an urgent purpose, such as a medical bill. Not only will the money be taxable in the year it is withdrawn, but the employee may also receive the ten percent additional withholding tax unless he or she is more than fifty-nine years and six months old and is totally and permanently disabled or meets the other IRS criteria for an exception to the rule. Again, we recommend that you do not withdraw the money, save that money because you will not have to pay those taxes or the ten percent if you do not meet the requirements.

Always have money set aside for an emergency, i.e. have a fund for emergencies and unforeseen events.

In the case of Roth IRAs, employee contributions may be withdrawn tax-free and without penalty at any time, but earnings will be taxable if the employee is less than fifty-nine years and six months old and has had the account for less than five years. And even if the employee is able to withdraw the tax-free money, it will diminish the retirement savings, which may be regretted later. Again, avoid at all costs withdrawing your savings from the account, leave it because in order to have more wealth in the future, we must make some sacrifices in the present.

2. Transfer it to an IRA

By transferring the money to an IRA at, for example, a brokerage firm or mutual fund company, the employee can avoid immediate taxes and maintain the tax-advantaged status of his or her account. In addition, the employee is likely to have a wider range of investment options in an IRA than with his or her employer's plan. This is a very good option and valid in case we change jobs.

The Internal Revenue Service has relatively strict rules about transfers and how they should be carried out and dealing with them can be costly. Usually, the financial institution that is online to receive the money will be more than happy to help with the process and avoid any false steps. As we have already mentioned, it is very important that we understand all the variables, understand the legality of what we want to do and if we are not sure, that we consult with a person specialized in the subject. We do not want to take false steps or have problems with the Internal Revenue Service. You should keep in mind, that money in a 401(k) or an IRA is generally protected from creditors.

If you are changing jobs, you also have the option of leaving the account with the former employer. This means that employers must allow an outgoing employee to maintain a 401(k) account indefinitely in his or her old plan, although the employee cannot make any further contributions to it. This generally applies to accounts with a value of at least five thousand U.S. dollars. If we have less than that amount, this option is not feasible. For smaller accounts, the employer can give the employee no choice but to move the money elsewhere. Then, if you have the opportunity, we recommend that you leave the money with your former employer unless you do not meet the value, in that case, move your money but keep contributing. Remember that this path will lead you to wealth and economic tranquility.

Leaving the 401(k) money where it is may make sense if the former employer's plan is well managed and the employee is satisfied with the investment options it offers. The danger is that employees who change jobs in the course of their careers may leave a trail of old 401(k) plans and may forget one or more of them. Your heirs may also be unaware of the existence of the accounts. For this reason, we recommend that you have a notebook, a folder on the computer or whatever suits you best, information about our accounts, where and in which companies or in which companies you have worked. This will keep you from losing any money and will help you to accumulate wealth. Remember to be tidy in your finances and never forget what plan you have.

On the other hand, if you don't have the amount of five thousand U.S. dollars and you don't meet the conditions, you must move the money to the new employer. Some companies allow new employees to transfer an old 401(k) to their own plan. As with an IRA rollover, this can maintain the tax-deferred status of the account and avoid immediate taxes. It may be a prudent decision if the employee is not comfortable making the investment decisions involved in administering a rollover IRA and prefers to leave some of that work to the administrator of the new plan.

Also, if the employee is approaching age seventy-six months, keep in mind that money that is in a 401(k) in the current employer is not subject to RMD. Moving the money will protect more retirement assets under that umbrella. Save as much as you can, make smart decisions, and you'll see how much wealth you can achieve. You can use different strategies to avoid having to pay so many taxes, so you'll have more cash available to spend, invest or save. Remember that these accounts hold the key to your future, the more you save, the more comfortably you will live in the future. Be clear about how old you want to be when you retire and how much money you need for your lifestyle. This will give you an idea of how much and how many years you need to save money, this means you need to know how much money you have to save each month in order to continue with the same lifestyle you currently have.

Chapter 8: What is an IRA? How does it benefit us?

We have been mentioning the IRA, what is it and what do we mean by that? We recommend that you reread and write down these definitions. This will give you a broader perspective of what suits you and what the real differences are and how they affect you., An individual Retirement Account (IRA) allows you to save money for retirement advantageously.

The growth of an individual retirement account (IRA) depends on many factors. It is largely based on the amount of money invested and the risk the investor is willing to take, which determines what type of investments are included in the account. Making regular contributions to the account also has a dramatic effect on performance. Take into account that we must have all the information about the risks related to our investments in order to make educated and informed decisions about our money and our future.

If I choose an IRA, will the contributions affect the IRA's growth? Yes, one really important factor that determines the growth of an IRA is how much we are contributing. Beginning in 2019, the IRA contributions have been limited to six thousand U.S. dollars a year. In 2018 for example, you could only contribute five thousand five hundred U.S. dollars annually, if you are under fifty years and six months, you can contribute seven thousand U.S. dollars if you are 50 years old or older (due to the additional one thousand U.S. dollars allowed through a recovery contribution). If six thousand US dollars are invested annually in an IRA with a return of five percent, we must consider that after thirty years, the account would be worth more than four hundred thousand dollars. The fact that interest can be reinvested and grow tax-free is really good for increasing wealth. Have you ever heard of the IRA before?

Are inflation and other factors such as the economy considered? Of course, to beat inflation, it is necessary to invest in riskier investment vehicles, such as individual stocks, index funds or mutual funds. IRAs may invest in a variety of securities offered by various entities: public corporations, general partnerships (GPs), limited partnerships (LPs), limited liability companies (LLPs), and limited liability companies (LLCs). Investments in IRAs that are related to these entities include stocks, corporate bonds, private equity and a limited number of derivative products. However, not all investments are eligible for an IRA; antiques or collectibles, life insurance and personal real estate, among others are not eligible. We need to emphasize   that there are different types of accounts and ways to save and acquire more money in IRAs, but this will depend on how much risk we want and are willing to take.

What is popular about IRAs? Which one is good for me? For example, stocks are a popular option for IRAs because the proceeds are basically additional contributions to the IRA. Stocks also grow IRAs through dividends and increases in stock prices. While no one can predict the future, the annual range of return on equity investments has historically been between eight percent and twelve percent. To be a little clearer, let's give you an example: by investing six thousand US dollars a year in a stock index fund for 30 years with an average yield of ten percent, you could see your account grow to more than one million dollars (although you need to take into account the impact of investment fees). With great potential to increase funds consistently over time with the magic of capitalization, it's clear why stocks almost always appear in IRA accounts. Are you surprised? A million dollars? Is that possible? We know that's what you're thinking, but yes, it's possible. It's all about knowing where and how to invest our money. If we follow different strategies and shortcuts, we can reduce our taxes and increase our capital. This is going to lead us to wealth without thinking about it and without much effort. Are you already starting to make your calculations? Start to plan and think where you will invest your money to increase your wealth.

Riskier investments, such as stocks, help increase IRAs more dramatically. More stable investments, such as bonds, are often included in IRAs to diversify and balance stock volatility with stable income. It's up to you to decide if it's worth taking that risk, don't forget to consider that you can lose money, but you can also gain money. This decision is personal, take as much time as you need to think about and analyze this.

Remember that an IRA is an account established at a financial institution that allows an individual to save for retirement with tax-free or tax-deferred growth. The 3 main types of IRAs have different advantages. You'll also have to decide which one is right for you. Let's start by explaining the different types of IRAs so that you can decide based on your current situation what might be the best option for you.

Traditional IRA: This is the one that makes contributions with money that you can deduct on your tax return, and any earnings can grow tax-deferred until you withdraw them in retirement. Many retirees are in a lower tax category than they were before, so tax deferral means money can be taxed at a lower rate. You'll need to review the amount of money you file for taxes and what's best for you.

On the other hand, the Roth IRA is where we can make contributions with money you've already paid taxes on (after taxes), and your money can potentially grow tax-free, with tax-free withdrawals at retirement, provided certain conditions are met. Take this into account, you must know how much you pay in taxes.

Now, the last option we will present is the Rollover IRA. This means that you are going to contribute "rollover" money from a qualified retirement plan to this traditional IRA. Transfers involve moving eligible assets from an employer-sponsored plan, such as a 401(k) or 403(b), to an IRA.

Whether you choose a traditional or Roth IRA, tax benefits allow your savings to grow or accumulate faster than in a taxable account. We know that so many definitions and so much information can be quite confusing and complicated. That's why we need to be clear about why we should invest in an IRA. We must be very clear about the benefits we could enjoy.

Do you know how much you have to save to retire? Many financial experts estimate that you may need up to eighty-five percent of your pre-retirement income when you retire. An employer-sponsored savings plan, such as a 401(k), may not be enough to accumulate the savings you need. Fortunately, you can contribute to both; a 401(k) and an IRA. You can keep your current savings in your employer-sponsored retirement plan, and you can gain access to a potentially wider range of investment options than your employer-sponsored plan.

You must remember and take advantage of potential tax-deferred growth and enjoy tax-free growth. We recommend that you try to contribute the maximum amount of money you can to your IRA each year to make the most of these savings. Be sure to control your investments and make the necessary adjustments, especially as retirement approaches and your goals change. Save more, prepare your budget and follow it, reduce your unnecessary expenses. Contribute more money to your retirement, increase your savings and your emergency fund. You never know when you might have an emergency and need that money.

Conclusion:

We recommend that you read the book again because of the technicality of the book. The first thing you need to do now is to know the actual amount of money you are paying in taxes; you can calculate how much money you could be saving once you have found a way to reduce your taxes. You need to know what you are spending on to analyze how you can reduce it.

As we have already explained, there are different strategies and different ways and shortcuts that will allow us to reduce the amount of taxes we are paying. You must always remember to consult a professional in order to make sure we are abiding the law. Remember there are certain steps you need to follow in order to taxes. Why is it a good idea to invest our money? Because we must reduce our taxes to the minimum, that is to say, as much as we can to be able to have more wealth in the future. Reducing our taxes will increase the amount of disposable income.

Make sure that you understand the strategies and shortcuts to reduce taxes using Cash Value Life Insurance, 1031 Real Estate Exchange, the 401k or the IRA.

Remember that Cash Value Insurance is a permanent life insurance that allows cash withdrawal, the 1031 Real

Estate Exchange allows you to avoid paying taxes on capital gains when you sell an investment property and reinvests the proceeds of the sale within certain time limits in a property or properties of a similar type and equal or greater value. We must take into account that the replacement property must be of equal or of greater value. This means that you must identify a replacement property for assets sold within forty-five days of the conclusion of the exchange within one hundred and eighty.

Remember that you must understand and follow the regulations. Review and learn the three-property rule, the two-hundred percent rule, and the ninety-five percent rule. The tax deferral provided by a 1031 exchange is a wonderful opportunity for investors. Although complex at some points, these complexities allow for great flexibility. This is not a procedure for an investor acting alone. Competent professional assistance is required in virtually every step. Remember that this can also be used in cases of inheritance, among others. We understand that it is complicated and technical, so we recommend that you work together with a professional.

On the other hand, do you have a pension? Are you saving money for your future? Are you currently working in a company with retirement plans? We recommend that you ask your employer about the 401(k) plan and see which one is right for you, which could be the traditional plan or the Roth plan. You should also consider your age, the variants of each plan, and we recommend that you keep the IRA in mind. Remember whatever you are choosing, it will be affected if you change Jobs., Your age and your income, among others. If you follow all of our strategies and shortcuts, you can lower your tax bill. By following some of the tips and strategies we have provided in this book, you will see your wealth increasing. You have to think about your retirement and your lifestyle, this will help you decide what plan suits you. Don't forget that you will have to elaborate your Budget in which you will have to include your income and, your expenses. We recommend that you reduce your expenses as much as you can and the amount of taxes that you pay. Review your subscriptions Spotify, Netflix have substitutes and you can reduce the amount of days a week you order take outs. Make a budget, lower your expenses, reduce your taxes and you'll see how it increases your wealth and your savings.

CPSIA information can be obtained
at www.ICGtesting.com
Printed in the USA
BVHW031022220922
647760BV00009B/41/J

9 781647 772239